How to Family Tree

by Gail Mack

HOUGHTON MIFFLIN HARCOURT
School Publishers

PHOTOGRAPHY CREDITS: Cover © image100/CORBIS. 1 © BananaStock/Jupiter Images. 4 © BananaStock/Jupiter Images. 5 (b) © CORBIS, (t) © Bettmann/CORBIS. 6 © image100/CORBIS. 7 © Masterfile (Royalty-Free Division). 14 (b) © Ariel Skelley/CORBIS, (t) Blend Images Photography/Veer.

Printed in China

ISBN-10: 0-547-25276-5
ISBN-13: 978-0-547-25276-6

11 12 13 0940 18 17 16 15 14 13
4500443494

What Is a Family Tree?

All of the people in your family are related to you. They are called your relatives. Some of the people in your family lived long ago.

A family tree is a way of showing the people in your family. The tree lists their names. The names hang down, like the leaves on a tree. Sometimes a family tree is big and shows the names of all your relatives. Sometimes it shows just a few.

If you want to make a family tree, start with the names of your mother's parents. Your mother and her relatives make up one side of the tree. Then show your father and his relatives. They make up the other side of the tree.

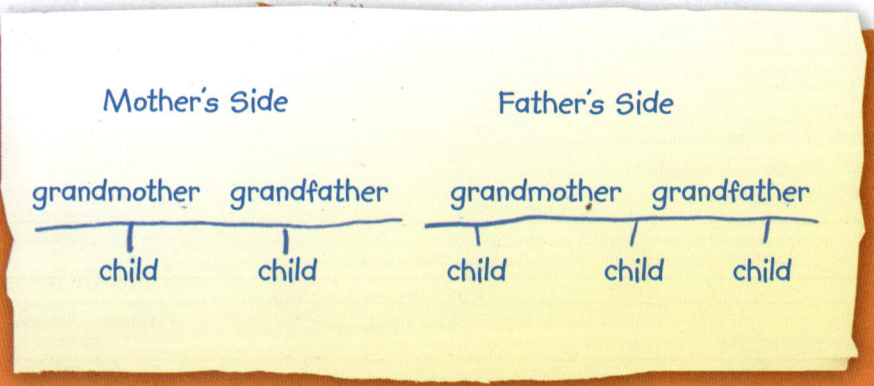

Who Is on a Family Tree?

Many people look carefully at their family tree. They hope to find an exciting relative from long ago. Sometimes people hope to learn that they are related to a king or queen who wore a royal <mark>crown</mark>!

This book will show you how to make a family tree. This tree will not list everyone in a family. It will not go back to kings and queens from long ago. On this family tree we will begin with grandparents.

Here is an example of a family tree!

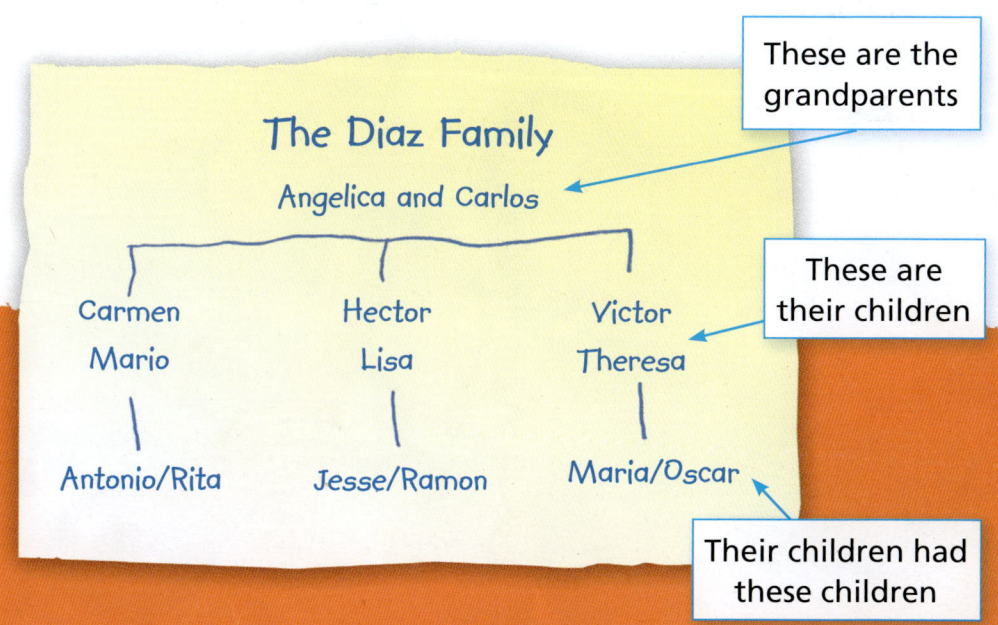

The Diaz Family

Angelica and Carlos

These are the grandparents

| Carmen | Hector | Victor |
| Mario | Lisa | Theresa |

These are their children

| Antonio/Rita | Jesse/Ramon | Maria/Oscar |

Their children had these children

Learn About Your Family

Do you want to make your own family tree? First, collect information about your family. Spend some time talking with your family. Talk with your parents, aunts, uncles, and cousins.

Sometimes families visit each other and tell stories. Some families like to sit on a porch and tell stories. Some families like to sit inside and tell stories. You can ask your family if anyone remembers family stories from long ago. These stories will help you learn about your family.

Look through photo albums together with your family and ask about the people in the photos. Do any of these people belong on your family tree?

Talk to older people in your family. Ask them about when they were young. Here are some questions to ask:

- Where did you live?
- What was school like?
- What games did you play when you were my age?
- Did you play the <mark>piano</mark> or any other instruments?
- What was happening in the world?

Keep a notebook with the title *My Family Tree*. You can write family stories down in your notebook. If you have a camera you can take photographs of the person telling the story.

Write the names of your family in your notebook. You might need help spelling or remembering a name. If you get <mark>stuck</mark>, ask someone for help.

Make Your Own Family Tree

Now you can use the information about your family. You can make your family tree. Follow these steps.

Step 1

Collect the materials you need to make your family tree.

Materials

- 1 poster board
- ruler
- pencil
- pen
- eraser
- green and brown markers
- list of names

Step 2

Use a ruler and a pencil to draw a straight line across the left side of the poster board. Write the names of your mother's parents on this line. These are your grandparents.

Step 3

Then draw another straight line across the right side of the poster board. Write the names of your father's parents on this line. These are your other grandparents.

My Family Tree

name of my
mother's parents
_____

name of my
father's parents
_____

Use your ruler to draw short lines hanging down from your grandparents' names. Draw one line for each of their children. Write their names under the lines.

Sometimes grandparents have many children. Sometimes they only have one child. How many aunts do you have? How many uncles?

On this family tree, the mother's family has two children and the father's family has three children. Your family tree might look different.

How many of your aunts and uncles are married? Write the name of the person they married. Write it underneath your aunt's or uncle's name.

Follow the model shown below. Write your mother's name where it says "my mother." Write your father's name where it says "my father." Do the same with other names in your family.

My Family Tree

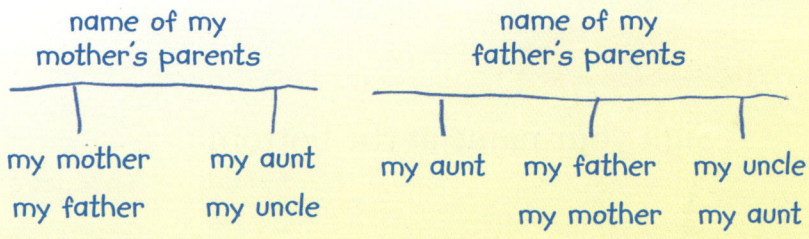

name of my mother's parents	name of my father's parents
my mother my aunt	my aunt my father my uncle
my father my uncle	my mother my aunt

On this family tree, some people are married and some people are not married.

Step 6

Write your name under your parents' names. Do you have brothers or sisters? Write their names here also.

Step 7

Use your pen to write over the penciled names. When you are finished, use your green marker to draw an outline that looks like a treetop around the top of the chart. Use a brown marker to add a tree trunk.

Step 8

Sign your name at the bottom!

My Family Tree

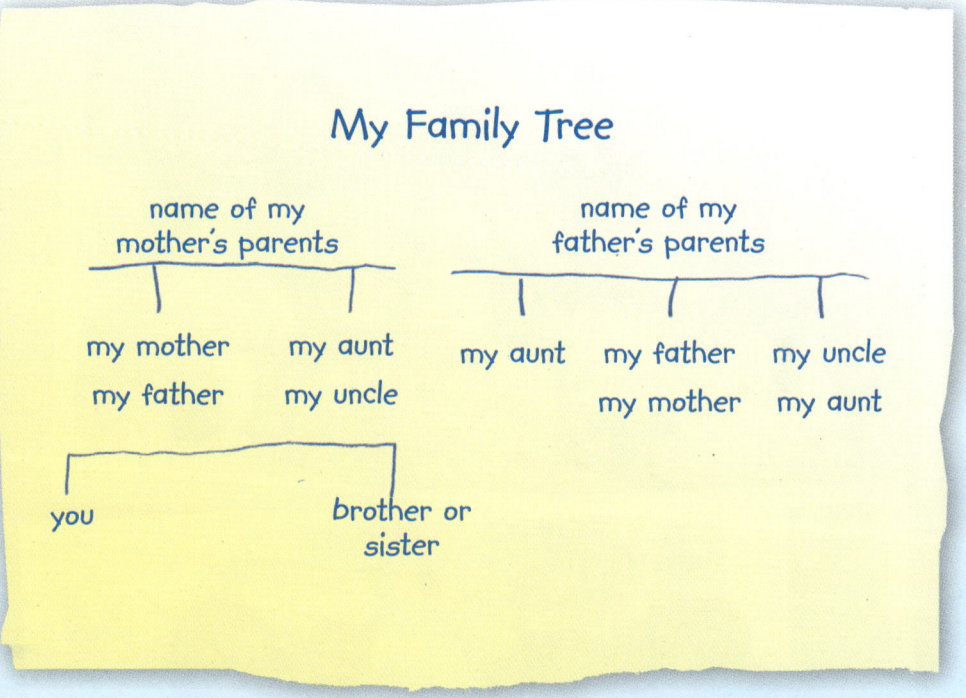

name of my
mother's parents

name of my
father's parents

my mother   my aunt   my aunt   my father   my uncle

my father   my uncle   my mother   my aunt

you   brother or
sister

Families Get Together

Share your family tree with your whole family!

Responding

✔ TARGET SKILL **Compare and Contrast**

Think about your family tree. Use a Venn diagram like this one to compare and contrast details about it.

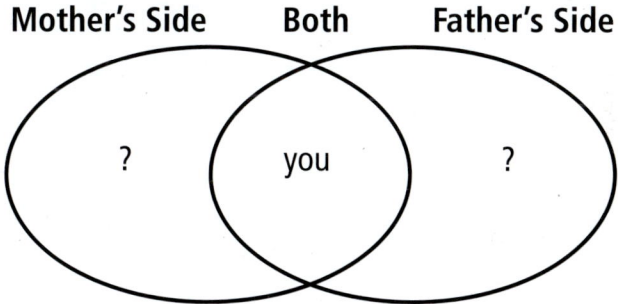

Mother's Side   Both   Father's Side

?   you   ?

 Write About It

Text to Text Have you read another book about families? Write a friendly letter to someone telling them about the book.

TARGET VOCABULARY

cousin	remembered
crown	spend
piano	stuck
porch	visit

EXPAND YOUR VOCABULARY

collect	penciled
grandparents	relatives

TARGET SKILL **Compare and Contrast** Tell how two things are alike or not.

TARGET STRATEGY **Question** Ask questions about what you are reading.

GENRE **Informational text** gives facts about a topic.